Common Core Lessons & Activities:
Indian Removal & the Trail of Tears

By Carole Marsh ©Carole Marsh/Gallopade
Published by Gallopade International, Inc.
Printed in the U.S.A. (Peachtree City, Georgia)

TABLE OF CONTENTS

G: Includes Graphic Organizer
GO: Graphic Organizer is also available 8½'
download at www.gallopade.com/clier
(numbers above correspond to the gra

Gold, Cotton, & Tribal Land

Read the text and answer the questions.

Native Americans (Indians) in the Southeast used the natural resources of the land long before European settlers came to America. They gathered fruits and nuts. They hunted game and fished. They planted beans, squash, and corn and used plants to make medicine. They believed that land was something to share. Many Native American tribes focused on the importance of community and sharing ownership of land. They did not believe that one person could own land.

European (white) settlers came to America with different beliefs about the land. Like the Indians, white settlers used the natural resources of the land to survive. However, they also believed that individuals should own land for the use of production and profit. Settlers thought the land should be used to grow crops to make money. Settlers grew cotton, tobacco, indigo, and other crops. As more settlers came, vast plantations and farms were established. Slowly, the European settlers <u>encroached</u> on Indian land, taking more and more of it by tricking, bribing, or forcing Indians away from their homelands. In the late 1820s, gold was discovered in northern Georgia on Cherokee lands. Treasure seekers flooded the area. More and more settlers wanted the Indians removed from the land. The U.S. government began to make plans for Indian removal.

1. Use clues in the text to define <u>encroached</u>.
2. What did settlers in the Southeast want to use land for? Why?
3. How did the discovery of gold on Cherokee lands affect the Cherokee people?
4. Describe each group's point of view to complete the chart.

Point of View	...about the purpose of land	...about their relationship to land
Native Americans		
European Settlers		

MAP ACTIVITY

Indian Land in the 1820s

Study the map and answer the questions.

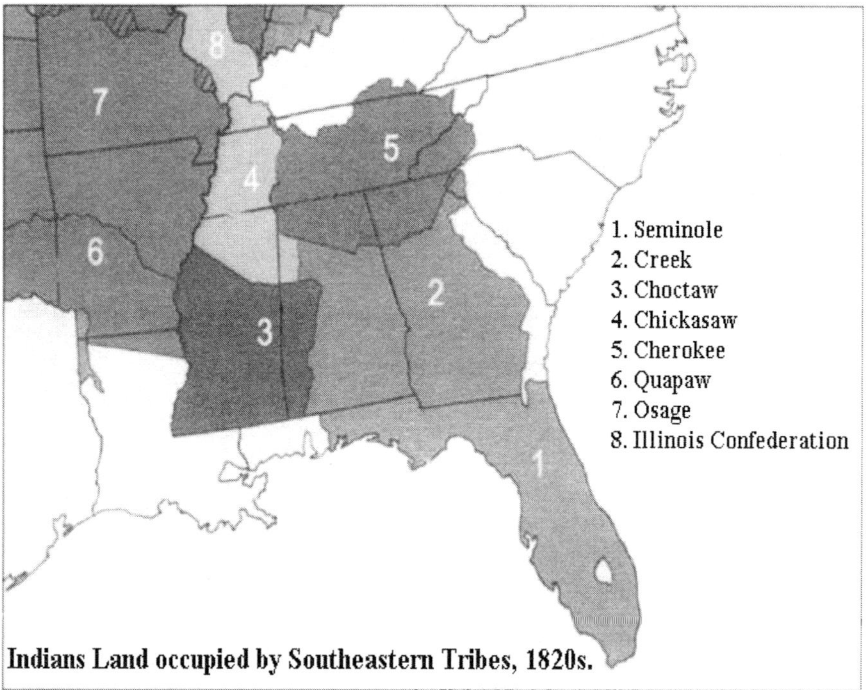

Courtesy of the U.S. Department of the Interior

1. What information does this map provide?
2. Use the map to determine whether each statement is **true** or **false**.

   _____The Chickasaw nation was the largest Indian tribe in 1820.

   _____The Seminole tribe was primarily confined to Florida.

   _____Georgia was primarily occupied by Creek and Choctaw tribes.
3. What can you infer about the population of the Southeastern United States in 1820?
4. Is the map better categorized as a map created in the 1800s or a map created in the 2000s? Explain.
5. Explain why the boundaries of most Indian nations do not fit the boundaries of the states.

READING INFORMATIONAL TEXT

Sequoyah and the Alphabet

Read the text, look at the Cherokee symbols, and answer the questions.

Before the arrival of European settlers, most Indian tribes told stories to pass their history and beliefs from one generation to the next. The settlers thought of Indians as savages because most Indian tribes did not have a written language. Indian clothing, speech, and religions were also different from those of the settlers. Some Indian tribes adopted the settlers' ways of farming, dressing, and speaking to be considered "civilized" in the eyes of European settlers.

One Cherokee Indian named Sequoyah thought that a written language would be useful for the Cherokee people. Therefore, Sequoyah invented the Cherokee alphabet. Sequoyah wanted his people to be able to send messages on paper, which the Indians called "talking leaves."

Some Cherokee leaders doubted an alphabet would be valuable, but Sequoyah did not give up. He worked for 12 years to develop the alphabet to represent his language. Although he did not speak English, Sequoyah borrowed an English alphabet as an example, and he completed the Cherokee alphabet in the early 1820s. The Cherokee tribe soon began publishing its own newspaper. They wrote the Cherokee Constitution in 1827 and published it in English and Cherokee.

1. Why did European settlers think Indians were savages?
2. What was Sequoyah's purpose for developing an alphabet?
3. Look at the Cherokee symbols. How are they similar to the alphabet used for English? Why? How are they different?
4. What effects did Sequoyah's alphabet have on the Cherokee tribe?

The Five Civilized Tribes

Use an online resource to identify the Five Civilized Tribes and key facts about each. Use the information to complete the graphic organizer.

Tribe:

Key Facts:

Tribe:

Key Facts:

Tribe:

Key Facts:

The Five Civilized Tribes

Tribe:

Key Facts:

Tribe:

Key Facts:

Dr. Worcester & Dr. Butler

Read the text and answer the questions.

In many states, Christian missionaries lived with the Indian tribes to teach Indians the ways of farming and introduce them to Christianity. Two missionaries, Dr. Samuel Worchester and Dr. Elizer Butler, resisted the Cherokee removal in Georgia. Georgia saw that the missionaries were an obstacle to Indian removal. Therefore, Georgia passed laws that the missionaries could not live on Indian land without permission from the governor.

Worcester and Butler did not ask permission and continued to live with the Cherokee illegally. They believed that the U.S government could not make laws about Indian land. Worcester and Butler also believed Indian tribes should be considered independent nations with their own laws.

In 1831, Georgia brought Worcester, Butler, and five other missionaries to court and sentenced them to four years of hard labor in state prison. Georgia's governor offered the men their freedom if they would leave the state, but Worcester and Butler refused. They appealed the case to the Supreme Court. In *Worcester v. Georgia,* Supreme Court Chief Justice John Marshall agreed with Worcester. The court released the missionaries from prison, and *Worcester v. Georgia* ruled that Indian tribes were nations with their own rights, governments, and laws.

Worcester v. Georgia was a victory against Indian removal, but it was not enough to stop white settlers. President Andrew Jackson, who had recently signed the Indian Removal Act, did not approve of Marshall's decision. Jackson famously said, "Justice Marshall has made his decision, now let him enforce it."

1. Why did Worcester and Butler live with the Indians?
2. Why did Georgia pass a law against missionaries living with Indians?
3. Why were Worcester and Butler sentenced to prison?
4. In your opinion, why did Georgia's governor offer to give Worcester and Butler their freedom if they left the state?
5. In what way was the Supreme Court's ruling in *Worcester v. Georgia* successful? In what way was it unsuccessful?

READING INFORMATIONAL TEXT

Chief William McIntosh

Read the text and answer the questions.

William McIntosh was the son of a Scotsman and a Creek Indian woman. He grew up among the Creeks, but he also spent time in his father's hometown of Savannah, Georgia, and spoke English fluently. Thus, McIntosh often had to choose between supporting the Creek Indians or siding with white Americans.

At the Battle of Horseshoe Bend during the War of 1812, McIntosh helped Andrew Jackson's army defeat the Lower Creek Indians and take their land. For his heroism, McIntosh was given the rank of general. However, many Creeks resented McIntosh for fighting against the Creeks and named him the "white warrior."

McIntosh believed it was best for Indians to assimilate, or change their ways to the ways of white men. McIntosh argued that Indians could not fight against the movement of white settlers. He wanted the Indians to sell their land while the U.S. government was willing to pay. "The white tide rises, we can't fight or stop it and if we don't sell, we will be cast aside, homeless and treated like animals without any place to go," he said.

Creek law said that no land could be given to the United States without the agreement of the entire Creek Nation. However, Chief McIntosh and six of the other chiefs signed the Treaty of Indian Springs on Feb. 12, 1825, selling Creek lands in Georgia for $200,000. Many Creeks saw McIntosh as a traitor, and McIntosh was killed in a violent attack a few months later.

1. How does being named a general reflect the white settlers' perspective of McIntosh?
2. How does the nickname "white warrior" reflect the Creek's perspective of McIntosh?
3. Use the text to explain the figurative phrase, "The white tide rises."
4. Rewrite McIntosh's quote in your own words to express its main idea.
5. In your opinion, was McIntosh more concerned with helping white Americans or Creek Indians? Cite evidence from the text to support your position.

READING INFORMATIONAL TEXT

President Andrew Jackson

Read the text and answer the questions.

Andrew Jackson (1767-1845) was born poor, but he grew up to become a successful lawyer, state legislator, and judge in Tennessee. Before he became President, Jackson became well known in the military and often fought against the Indian nations.

As a major general in the Tennessee militia, Jackson defeated the Creek Indians and took their land at The Battle of Horseshoe Bend in 1814. This victory opened up Creek land for settlers in Georgia and Alabama. Jackson became a national hero the next year when he led the United States to victory over the British in the Battle of New Orleans. In 1817, Jackson won battles against the Seminoles in the Spanish territory of Florida. Despite his military actions, Jackson did show some compassion for Indians. He even adopted a Creek Indian son named Lyncoya after the boy's mother was killed during Jackson's battle with the Red Sticks tribe of Creeks during the Battle of Talladega.

Andrew Jackson became the nation's seventh president in 1828 and was elected to a second term in 1832. He gained the nickname "Old Hickory" because of his tough, aggressive personality and political policies. Most famously, Jackson did not approve of Indian culture, and believed that the land could be better used by the American people. During his presidency, he was a strong supporter of the Indian Removal Act, which forced thousands of Native Americans to leave their homes and move west.

1. Use the text to make 3-5 inferences about Andrew Jackson's character. Cite evidence from the text to support each inference.
2. How did Jackson's victory at the Battle of Horseshoe Bend affect the Creek Indians? How did it affect settlers in Georgia and Alabama?
3. Is "Old Hickory" an appropriate nickname for Andrew Jackson? Cite evidence from the text.
4. How did Andrew Jackson's presidency affect Native Americans?
5. Imagine you are Lyncoya. Write a letter to Andrew Jackson expressing your opinion of his actions against the Indians.

PRIMARY SOURCE ANALYSIS

The Great White Father

This engraving of Andrew Jackson from the 1830s depicts Andrew Jackson as a father to the Native Americans.

Look at the cartoon and answer the questions.

1. Describe what you see. What details do you notice first?
2. A. Who is represented by the person marked with arrow A?
   B. Who is represented by the people marked with arrows B?
3. What is the main idea conveyed by this cartoon?
4. What symbols or words communicate the main idea?
5. Is the cartoon's representation of A negative or positive? Explain.
6. From what point of view is this cartoon depicted?
7. Discuss the political cartoon as a class. Expand your answers to the previous questions based on new insight and ideas shared.

Indian Removal Act

Read the text and answer the questions.

Settlers moving into the southeastern U.S. wanted land that belonged to the Indians. The movement of these U.S. settlers threatened the land, laws, and governments of the Cherokee, Creek, Choctaw, Chickasaw, and Seminole Indians.

The U.S federal and state governments saw the Indians as a problem. Settlers wanted to claim Indian land and expand the United States for farming. The Indian tribes tried many ways to protect their lands, but the U.S. government used laws, treaties, and warfare to take the Indian's land.

The Indian Removal Act of 1830 was a highly influential law that allowed Congress to trade land with the Indians. Jackson used the Indian Removal Act to trade land in the Louisiana Purchase in the west to the Indians for their homelands in the southeastern U.S. President Andrew Jackson told Congress that the new Indian Territory would belong to the Indians as long as they lived there.

Some Indian tribes moved soon after the Indian Removal Act was passed. However, many tribes, including many of the Cherokee people, refused to leave their homelands. After the Treaty of New Echota, the U.S. Government forcefully relocated the Cherokee to Indian Territory in 1838. The journey from the southeastern U.S. to Indian Territory in the west was a long and difficult path through wilderness. Over 4,000 Cherokee Indians died on the journey, and the Cherokee people named it "The trail where we cried," which later became known as the Trail of Tears.

1. Why did U.S. settlers want to remove the Indians from the Southeastern United States?
2. What power did the Indian Removal Act give Congress?
3. How did the Louisiana Purchase relate to the Indian Removal Act?
4. Identify the cause and effect relationship between the Indian Removal Act and the Trail of Tears.
5. Why is the Indian relocation to Indian Territory called the Trail of Tears?

COMPARISON OF PRIMARY SOURCES

Jackson vs. Cherokee

Read the quotations and answer the questions. Then complete the writing prompt.

"What good man would prefer a country covered with forests and ranged by a few thousand savages to our extensive Republic, studded with cities, towns, and prosperous farms embellished with all the improvements which art can devise or industry execute, occupied by more than 12,000,000 happy people, and filled with all the blessings of liberty, civilization, and religion?"

—Andrew Jackson
Message to Congress on Indian Removal (1830)

"We, the great mass of the people think only of the love we have for our land for...we do love the land where we were brought up. We will never let our hold on this land go... To let it go will be like throwing away...[our] mother that gave...[us] birth."

—Cherokee Legislative Council in New Echota (1830)

1. What is the common theme shared between these quotations?
2. Summarize the point of view expressed in each quotation.
3. What strategies does each speaker use to promote his point of view? Provide examples.
4. What can you infer about Andrew Jackson's opinion of Indian culture? What words or phrases support your conclusion?

Writing Prompt

A. Choose the perspective of a Cherokee Indian or United States settler and write a short speech to your people. State your opinion on the uses of land. Use the points of view expressed in the quotations to support your position.

B. Edit and revise your speech. Vary sentence structure, include transitions, use impactful words and literary devices, and proofread.

C. Give your speech to the class. Can your audience accurately determine whether you are speaking as a Cherokee or a settler?

March to the

Complete the graphic organizer with people and events that played a role in Indian removal from the southeastern United States. Explain the effect each had on Native Americans.

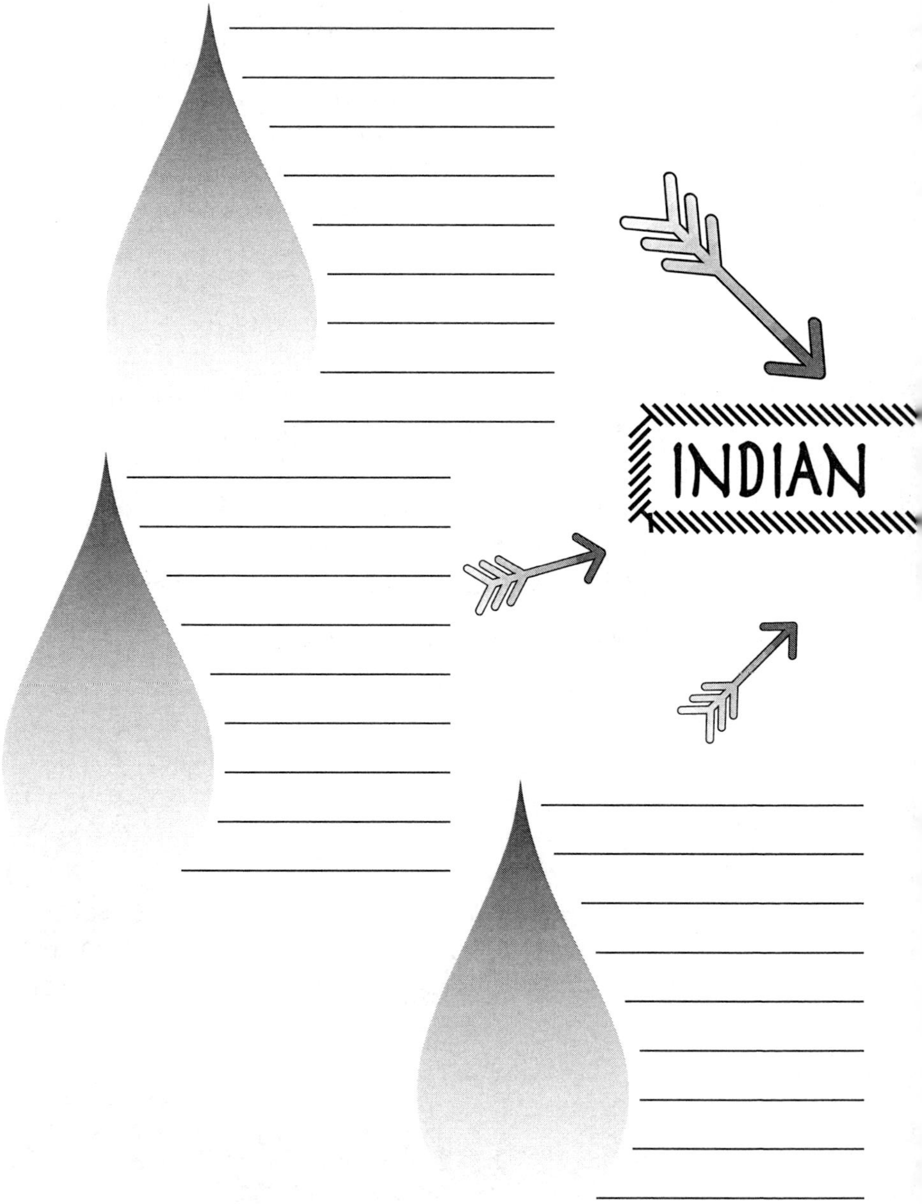

Trail of Tears

TERRITORY

Trail of Tears Vocabulary

Use a dictionary and other resources to complete the graphic organizer for each vocabulary word.

allegiance	cede	disenfranchise	internment	sovereign
assimilate	civilized	encroach	negotiate	treaty

WORD

DEFINITION

SYNONYM

ANTONYM

SENTENCE

Pre-Removal Problems

Use the graphic organizer to analyze one or more pre-Trail of Tears problems.

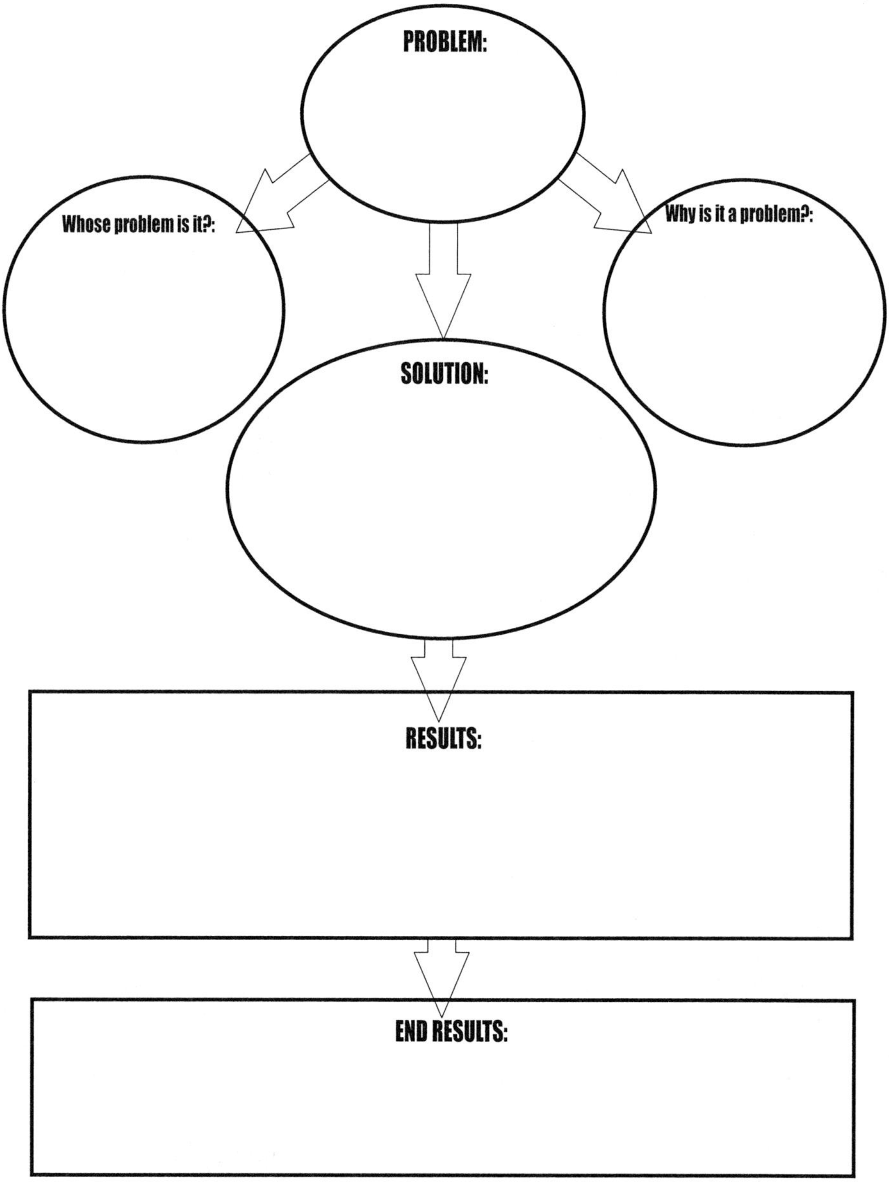

PRIMARY SOURCE ANALYSIS

Cherokee Chief John Ross

Look at the portrait of the Cherokee Chief John Ross and answer the questions.

Courtesy of Wikipedia

1. Describe Cherokee Chief John Ross based upon his portrait.
2. What does John Ross' portrait indicate about his heritage?
3. What does John Ross' portrait indicate about his education?
4. What is the significance of the paper in John Ross' hand?
5. How does John Ross' portrait represent the Cherokee Nation as one of the Five Civilized Tribes?
6. Use an online resource to compare and contrast John Ross' portrait to the portraits of President Andrew Jackson and Shawnee leader Tecumseh. Which leader does Ross resemble more? Discuss why.

READING INFORMATIONAL TEXT

Treaty of New Echota

Read the text and answer the questions.

In the late 1820s, Cherokee Chief John Ross and Cherokee leader Major Ridge believed that the Cherokee tribe and land should be independent from the United States. Together, they formed the Cherokee Nation. Even though the leaders made a "civilized" Cherokee nation, white settlers still wanted their land.

After the Indian Removal Act was passed, Ross fought back politically and legally to save the Cherokee lands. On the other hand, Major Ridge and his followers wished to negotiate and make agreements with the U.S. government. In December 1835, Major Ridge and 20 other Cherokees signed the Treaty of New Echota without Ross' permission. In this treaty, Ridge agreed to sell all Cherokee land in Georgia to the U.S government for $4.5 million and promised the Cherokee would relocate to the Indian Territory west of the Mississippi River. President Andrew Jackson signed the treaty and Congress ratified it.

The Cherokee people divided over the Treaty of New Echota. Ridge and his followers were the first Cherokee to depart for the Indian Territory west of the Mississippi River. However, Chief Ross and most of the Cherokees stayed in Georgia. Chief Ross argued that the Treaty of New Echota was unlawful. None of the Cherokee Council leaders signed the treaty, and Major Ridge's group did not represent the entire Cherokee nation. Despite Ross' arguments, General Winfield Scott and 7,000 U.S. soldiers marched to Georgia in May, 1838. The soldiers forcefully removed the remaining Cherokee from the state, and sent them on the Trail of Tears.

1. How were John Ross and Major Ridge similar? How were they different?

2. Analyze each statement and identify it as either a **cause** or **effect** of the Treaty of New Echota:
   _____The Indian Removal Act is passed.
   _____Major Ridge and his followers willingly depart for new land out west.
   _____Major Ridge wants to make agreements with the U.S. government.
   _____The Cherokee people are divided.
   _____U.S. soldiers forcefully remove the Cherokee from their land in 1838.

3. Why did John Ross believe the Treaty of New Echota was unlawful?

PRIMARY SOURCE ANALYSIS

John Ross' Speech

This speech is an excerpt from John Ross' address to the Iroquois League of Indian Tribes on behalf of the Cherokee tribe.

Read the text and answer the questions.

"Ever since [the whites came] we have been made to drink of the bitter cup of humiliation; treated like dogs...our country and the graves of our Fathers torn from us...through a period of upwards of 200 years, rolled back, nation upon nation [until] we find ourselves fugitives, vagrants and strangers in our own country....

The existence of the Indian nations as distinct independent communities within the limits of the United States seems to be drawing to a close.... You are aware that our Brethren, the Choctaws, Chickasaws and Creeks of the South have severally disposed of their country to the United States and that a portion of our own Tribe have also emigrated West of the Mississippi—but that the largest portion of our Nation still remain firmly upon our ancient domain.... Our position there may be compared to a solitary tree in an open space, where all the forest trees around have been prostrated by a furious tornado."

1. A. What is the overall tone of the text?
   B. How does the author's choice of words create that tone?
2. Write an appropriate title to convey the main idea of John Ross' speech.
3. Is the phrase, "drink from the bitter cup of humiliation," figurative or literal? Explain.
4. Use the text to identify who or what is being described:

   ___________"our country and graves of our Fathers," "our ancient domain"

   ___________"our Bretheren"

   ___________"all the forest trees around"

   ___________"a solitary tree in an open space"

   ___________"a furious tornado"
5. What can you infer about the author's opinion of white settlers? Cite evidence to support your conclusion.

Events Leading to the Trail of Tears

Put these events in chronological order on the graphic organizer.

Treaty of New Echota	Cherokees forced on the Trail of Tears	Indian Removal Act passed	Louisiana Purchase	Election of President Andrew Jackson
Discovery of gold in Georgia	Cherokee arrive in Indian Territory	William McIntosh cedes Creek land	President Andrew Jackson re-elected	*Worcester v. Georgia*

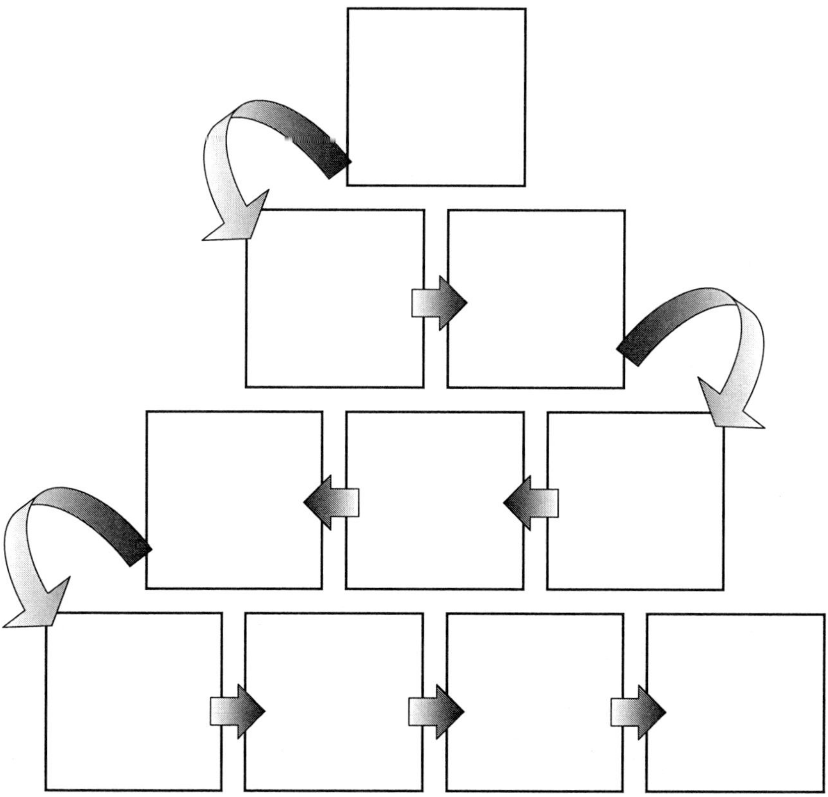

COMPARISON OF PRIMARY SOURCES

Accounts of the Trail of Tears

Read the excerpt and look at the painting. Then answer the questions.

"I saw helpless Cherokees arrested and dragged from their homes, and driven at the bayonet point into the stockades. And in the chill of a drizzling rain on an October morning, I saw them loaded like cattle or sheep into six hundred and forty-five wagons and started toward the west.

One can never forget the sadness and solemnity of that morning. Chief John Ross led in prayer and when the bugle sounded and the wagons started rolling many of the children rose to their feet and waved their little hands good-by to their mountain homes, knowing they were leaving them forever. Many of these helpless people did not have blankets and many of them had been driven from their home barefooted.

On the morning of November the 17th we encountered a terrific sleet and snow storm with freezing temperatures and from that day until we reached the end of the fateful journey on March the 26th, 1839, the sufferings of the Cherokees were awful. The trail of the exiles was a trail of death. They had to sleep in the wagons and on the ground without fire. And I have known as many as twenty-two of them to die in one night of pneumonia due to ill treatment, cold, and exposure. Among this number was the beautiful Christian wife of Chief John Ross. This noble hearted woman died a martyr to childhood, giving her only blanket for the protection of a sick child."

—Army Interpreter Private John G. Burnett's first-hand description the Cherokee Trail of Tears,1838-1839, told in 1890.

PART A: Use the text to answer the questions.

1. Make at least three inferences about the author of this text. Support each inference with evidence from the text.
2. Did the Cherokee people relocate willingly? Cite evidence.
3. How does the author characterize John Ross' wife? Why?
4. Cite evidence from the text to support the author's statement, "The trail of the exiles was a trail of death."

The Trail of Tears *was painted by Robert Lindneux in 1942.*

PART B: Analyze the painting to answer the questions.

5. What do you notice first? List 3-5 other observations from the painting and discuss.
6. Explain the significance of the setting of this painting.
7. What can you infer from the painting about the ways Indians traveled along the Trail of Tears?
8. What inferences can you make from the painting about life on the Trail of Tears? Cite evidence from the painting to support your inferences.

PART C: Use the text and the painting to answer the questions.

9. List at least 5 similarities and differences between the text and the painting.
10. Compare and contrast the points of view of each source. Consider the date of each source in your answer.
11. In your opinion, which source is more effective at depicting life on the Trail of Tears? Why?

BONUS: In small groups, use an online resource to compile 5 images representing the Trail of Tears. Use presentation technology to present and explain your images in the form of a slideshow. Discuss as a class.

Life and Death on the Trail

Read the text and answer the questions.

Tribe	Dates of Removal	# of Indians Removed	# of Deaths Along the Trail
Choctaw	1831-1833	about 12,500	about 2,500 (cholera, dysentery)
Creek	1834-1837	about 15,000	about 3,500 (disease)
Chickasaw	1837-1847	over 3,000	500-800 (dysentery and smallpox)
Cherokee	1836-1838	about 18,000	about 4,000 (pneumonia, whooping cough, dysentery, cholera, and starvation)
Seminole	Seminole wars from 1832-1842 Removal in 1842	about 3,000	unknown number (death mostly from warfare resisting removal)

1. What types of information does this chart provide?
2. Which tribes had the highest number of deaths from removal? Why?
3. What can you infer from the data about the quality of life on the trail?
4. What can you infer about the results of the Seminole wars? Explain.
5. Compare and contrast the data about each tribe. What similarities did most tribes share? Which tribe's experience was most unlike the rest?

MAP ACTIVITY

Tracing the Cherokee Trails

Look at the map and answer the questions.

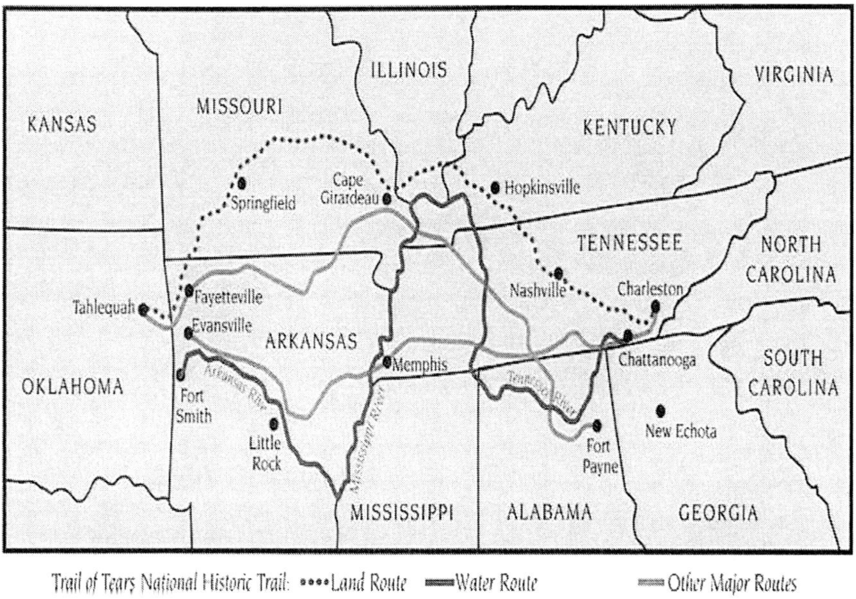

Courtesy of Wikipedia

1. What information does this map provide?
2. What areas did the Cherokee depart from? Where did their journey end?
3. Explain why the solid black route is not as direct as the other routes.
4. What details from the map support the idea that the Cherokee nation was deeply divided?
5. What can you infer about the date this map was made? Explain.

Writing Prompt

The Five Civilized Tribes traveled many different trails to the Indian Territory, but each group encountered similar hardships. In small groups, choose a specific tribe. Use an online resource to gather information about the tribe's journey west.

Summarize your information in the form of a visual and oral presentation and share with your class. Then compare and contrast the experiences of different tribes.

Correlations to Common Core State Standards

For your convenience, correlations are listed page-by-page and for the entire book!

This book is correlated to the Common Core State Standards for English Language Arts grades 3-8, and to Common Core State Standards for Literacy in History, Science, & Technological Subjects grades 6-8.

Correlations are highlighted in gray.

PAGE #	READING *Includes:* RI: Reading Informational Text RH: Reading History	WRITING *Includes:* W: Writing WHST: Writing History, Science, & Technology	LANGUAGE *Includes:* L: Language LF: Language Foundational Skills	SPEAKING & LISTENING *Includes:* SL: Speaking & Listening
2	RI RH . **1** **2** **3** **4** 5 6 7 8 9 **10**	W WHST . 1 2 3 4 5 6 7 8 9 10	L LF . 1 2 3 **4** 5 **6**	SL . 1 2 3 4 5 6
3	RI RH . 1 2 3 4 5 6 **7** 8 9 **10**	W WHST . 1 2 3 4 5 6 7 8 9 10	L LF . 1 2 3 4 5 6	SL . 1 2 3 4 5 6
4	RI RH . **1** **2** 3 4 **5** 6 **7** 8 9 **10**	W WHST . 1 2 3 4 5 6 7 8 9 10	L LF . 1 2 3 4 5 6	SL . 1 2 3 4 5 6
5	RI RH 1 2 3 4 5 6 7 8 **9** **10**	W WHST 1 2 3 4 5 6 **7** **8** **9** **10**	L LF 1 2 3 4 5 6	SL 1 2 3 4 5 6
6	RI RH . **1** **2** 3 4 5 6 7 8 9 **10**	W WHST . 1 2 3 4 5 6 7 8 9 10	L LF . 1 2 3 4 5 6	SL . 1 2 3 4 5 6
7	RI RH . **1** **2** 3 4 5 6 7 8 9 **10**	W WHST . **1** 2 3 4 5 6 7 8 9 10	L LF . 1 2 3 4 **5** **6**	SL . 1 2 3 4 5 6
8	RI RH . **1** **2** 3 4 5 6 7 8 9 **10**	W WHST . 1 2 **3** 4 5 6 7 8 9 **10**	L LF . 1 2 3 4 5 6	SL . 1 2 3 4 5 6
9	RI RH . 1 2 3 4 5 6 **7** 8 9 **10**	W WHST . 1 2 3 4 5 6 7 8 9 10	L LF . 1 2 3 4 5 6	SL . **1** 2 3 4 5 **6**
10	RI RH . **1** **2** 3 4 **5** 6 7 8 9 **10**	W WHST . 1 2 3 4 5 6 7 8 9 10	L LF . 1 2 3 4 5 6	SL . 1 2 3 4 5 6
11	RI RH . **1** **2** 3 4 **5** 6 7 **8** 9 **10**	W WHST . **1** 2 3 **4** **5** 6 7 8 9 10	L LF . 1 2 3 4 5 6	SL . 1 2 3 **4** 5 **6**
12-13	RI RH . 1 2 **3** 4 **5** 6 7 8 9 **10**	W WHST . 1 2 3 4 5 6 7 8 9 10	L LF . 1 2 3 4 5 6	SL . 1 2 3 4 5 6
14	RI RH . 1 2 3 **4** 5 6 7 8 9 **10**	W WHST . 1 2 3 4 5 6 7 **8** 9 **10**	L LF . 1 2 3 **4** 5 **6**	SL . 1 2 3 4 5 6
15	RI RH . 1 2 3 4 **5** 6 7 8 9 **10**	W WHST . 1 2 3 4 5 6 7 8 9 10	L LF . 1 2 3 4 5 6	SL . 1 2 3 4 5 6
16	RI RH . 1 2 3 4 **5** 6 **7** 8 9 **10**	W WHST . 1 2 3 4 5 6 **7** 8 9 **10**	L LF . 1 2 3 4 5 6	SL . 1 2 3 **4** 5 **6**
17	RI RH . 1 **2** 3 4 5 6 7 8 9 **10**	W WHST . 1 2 3 4 5 6 7 8 9 10	L LF . 1 2 3 4 5 6	SL . 1 2 3 4 5 6
18	RI RH . **1** **2** 3 4 5 6 7 **8** 9 **10**	W WHST . 1 2 3 4 5 6 7 8 9 10	L LF . 1 2 3 4 **5** **6**	SL . 1 2 3 4 5 6
19	RI RH . 1 2 3 4 **5** 6 7 8 9 **10**	W WHST . 1 2 3 4 5 6 7 8 9 10	L LF . 1 2 3 4 5 6	SL . 1 2 3 4 5 6
20-21	RI RH . **1** **2** 3 4 **5** **6** **7** **8** **9** **10**	W WHST . 1 2 3 4 5 **6** **7** **8** **9** **10**	L LF . 1 2 3 4 5 6	SL . **1** 2 3 **4** **5** **6**
22	RI RH . 1 2 3 4 **5** 6 **7** 8 9 **10**	W WHST . 1 2 3 4 5 6 7 8 9 10	L LF . 1 2 3 4 5 6	SL . 1 2 3 4 5 6
23	RI RH . 1 2 3 4 **5** 6 **7** 8 9 **10**	W WHST . 1 **2** 3 **4** 5 **6** **7** **8** **9** **10**	L LF . 1 2 3 4 5 6	SL . 1 **2** 3 **4** **5** **6**
COMPLETE BOOK	RI RH . **1** **2** **3** **4** **5** **6** **7** **8** **9** **10**	W WHST . **1** **2** **3** **4** **5** **6** **7** **8** **9** **10**	L LF . 1 2 3 **4** **5** **6**	SL . **1** **2** 3 **4** **5** **6**

For the complete Common Core standard identifier, combine your grade + "." + letter code above + "." + number code above.

In addition to the correlations indicated here, the activities may be adapted or expanded to align to additional standards and to meet the diverse needs of your unique students!